First published in Great Britain by Brockhampton Press,
a member of the Hodder Headline Group,
20 Bloomsbury Street, London WC1B 3QA

Copyright © 1998 Brockhampton Press

All rights reserved. No part of this publication may be
reproduced, stored in a retrieval system, or transmitted, in any form or by any
means, without the prior written permission of the
copyright holder.

ISBN 1 86019 313 7

Created and produced by Flame Tree Publishing,
part of The Foundry Creative Media Company Limited,
The Long House, Antrobus Road, Chiswick, London W4 5HY

Special thanks to
Kate Brown and Kelley Doak for their work on this series

Printed and bound in U.A.E.

Coleridge
Lyrical Romantic

Written and Compiled by
K. E. SULLIVAN

Contents

INTRODUCTION 6
AUTHOR'S NOTE 12
CHRONOLOGY 13

To the Autumnal Moon 14
Youth and Age 16
To the Nightingale 18
Pain 19
This Lime-Tree Bower My Prison 20
The Rime of the Ancient Mariner 25
Kubla Khan 56
The Exchange 59
Frost at Midnight 60
Song 63
Christabel – extract 64
Psyche 75
The Pains of Sleep 76
Recollections of Love 78
Sonnet: To the River Otter 81
An Invocation 82
Genevieve 84
Epitaph 86
Desire 86
Work Without Hope 87
Lines on a Friend 89
On Donne's Poetry 91

INDEX TO FIRST LINES 92
NOTES ON ILLUSTRATIONS 94

LYRICAL ROMANTIC

5

Introduction

I can contemplate nothing but parts, and parts are all little! My mind feels as if it ached to behold and know something great, something one and indivisible. And it is only in the faith of that, that rocks or waterfalls, mountains or caverns, give me the sense of sublimity or majesty!
Samuel Taylor Coleridge, 1797

Coleridge was the great intellect of the Romantic movement, a fabulously witty, inventive and imaginative poet whom Wordsworth called 'The only wonderful man I ever met'. There was a freshness, an immediacy to his writing which sets him apart from his contemporaries, and that work is characterized by an exotic imagery that is both haunting and reflective of his intense preoccupation with feeling, knowing, daydreaming and reverie.

Samuel Taylor Coleridge was born on 21 October 1772 in Ottery St Mary in Devonshire. He was the youngest of ten children born to John Coleridge, a vicar and headmaster who died in 1781. From 1782 to 1791 Coleridge attended Christ's Hospital School in the City of London as a charity scholar, and there he proved to be an excellent student, far surpassing his peers with the breadth of his academic skill and imagination. As a child he had mastered the Bible, and books like *The Arabian Nights* and it is not surprising that he revelled in the acquisition of learning, and found great pleasure in study. He went on to Jesus College in Cambridge, where he was equally known for his brilliance and his corruption – he lived highly, drank deeply of life and every hedonistic pleasure. His pre-occupations placed him seriously in debt, and he cut short his education to travel under an assumed name to London, where he enlisted in the 15th Light Dragoons. After several months, he grew tired of what he had perceived to be a somewhat glamorous career, and his brother arranged for

LYRICAL ROMANTIC

him to be discharged. His return to Cambridge was inglorious, for he could no longer concentrate in the confines of structured education, and he left again, stimulated by political theory, particularly that presented by the French Revolution, and by the world of nature which beckoned.

He travelled to Wales with Joseph Hucks, a fellow undergraduate, and met the poet Robert Southey. The two men shared a utopian ideology and planned to set up a community, called a pantisocracy, in America. Lack of funds put paid to this project, but the two men carried on a friendship from which both acquired enormous inspiration. Coleridge went to live with Southey in Bristol, until they fell out in September of 1795. Coleridge had already met the sister of Southey's fiancée, Sara Fricker, and they married in October of 1795 and went to live in Clevedon on the Bristol Channel. Coleridge lectured on politics and religion in Bristol, his first volume of poetry appeared in April of the following year, and several months later his first son was born.

Coleridge took great pleasure in walking, and in the natural world. Roger Hudson, author of *Coleridge Among the Lakes and Mountains*, wrote, 'He is a connoisseur of water — reflections in it, the flicker of light on the surface of tarns and lakes, the motion of waterfalls, the squalls of rain and banks of mist on mountains, particularly in his beloved Lake Country ... Like his contemporary, the painter J.M.W. Turner, Coleridge was trying to get down on paper, on a flat surface, that quintessential British concern, the weather.'

From Bristol Coleridge and his family moved to Nether Storey, funded by the well-known tannery Thomas Poole, who shared Coleridge's political views, and Coleridge's second volume of poems appeared in May of 1797. Coleridge's publisher was Joseph Cottle, who also published Wordsworth, and the two men met in the spring of 1797. Dorothy and William Wordsworth left their home in Dorset to move closer to Coleridge and his young family, and the two men formed a poetical alliance which was one of the greatest in the history of literature.

The year 1797 marked the beginning of one of Coleridge's most prolific periods, and that which has attracted the most critical acclaim. *Kubla Khan* was written, and *The Rime of the Ancient Mariner* begun. *Frost at Midnight*, *Fears in Solitude* and *Christabel* were also produced over the next year, works for which Coleridge is most remembered. It was once said about his poetry: 'All that he did excellently might be bound up in twenty pages, but it should be bound in pure gold.'

Coleridge was financed by Tom and Josiah Wedgwood, the pottery manufacturers, and he was able to concentrate on his poetry. Wordsworth and Coleridge had an idea for a co-operative volume of poetry, which they would call *Lyrical Ballads*, and after his second son Berkeley was born in May of 1798, Coleridge travelled to Germany with the Wordsworths where he remained for ten months, eventually brought home by the death of his baby son.

Coleridge befriended Southey once again upon his return to England, and after a brief visit with his wife, he left once again to see old friends, particularly Wordsworth who was staying in Durham with friends Tom Hutchinson, and his three sisters. Wordsworth himself eventually married Mary Hutchinson, and Coleridge fell hopelessly in love with Sara Hutchinson, who pledged her feelings in return.

He returned to his wife, although only for short spells, and eventually took lodgings in London, producing reams of articles for the *Morning Post* in order to supplement his pension from the Wedgwoods. He moved to the Lake District with his family in order to be closer to the Wordsworths, and here his son Derwent was born, in September 1880. Wordsworth and Coleridge planned the second edition of *Lyrical Ballads*, in which *Christabel* was to appear. Wordsworth, however, had a change of heart and vetoed its inclusion, an act which threw Coleridge into an unhealthy depression and provided him with a more profound excuse for his liberal intake of drugs.

Throughout these years, Coleridge drew enormous power from daydreaming, a habit which was accentuated by his use of drugs, in particular opium, to relieve the pain of neuralgia. This use grew to an addiction which caused the poet great personal difficulties – deep sadnesses, erratic behaviour and vagueness – and although some of his best works are those in which the imagination and fancy are expressed in an almost opiated way, there is evidence that his great creative power was suppressed by his abuses. Certainly the decision not to include *Christabel* in the second edition of *Lyrical Ballads* was responsible for a breakdown in his health, and many believe that his work never reached that supremely philosophical expression of the imagination that his earlier work had embodied. His depression is manifested in 'Dejection: An Ode', which was based on his tormented 'Letter to Sara Hutchinson', written in 1802, the same year.

Coleridge experimented with narrative verse, and had achieved extraordinary success with *The Rime of the Ancient Mariner*, four years earlier. In this, as his biographer Martin Corner notes, 'Coleridge insists on the indivisible nature of being, on the unity of the human with the non-human, the ethical with the aesthetic, the material with the spiritual. At the heart of the power is the power to love to unite human consciousness with God-in-Nature, in a visionary unity which Coleridge, as a schoolboy had found in the seventeenth-century mystic Boehme.'

Coleridge continued to see Sara Hutchinson, although it is unclear whether they were able to consummate their grand passions for one another. He travelled a great deal, intermittently nursed by his friends the Wordsworths and Charles Lamb and his wife, and continuing to forge a career as a journalist. His wife moved in with her sister and Robert Southey, and Coleridge left to travel abroad. On 14 January

1804 he headed on foot to London, and on to Malta and Italy. He acted as Secretary to the High Commissioner of Malta until September 1804, and then moved on to Rome and Florence. He returned to England at the request of Wordsworth, to stay in Leicestershire at the house of Sir George Beaumont, but he left there to lecture at the Royal Institution in London.

Coleridge wrote little poetry after 1807, but his works of prose were both important, unique and high-minded. He was a prolific and highly regarded journalist. His *Biographia Literaria*, is a unique analysis of the nature of poetry and the principles of criticism, and he achieved enormous attention for his *Lectures on Shakespeare*, which rank him among the greatest of the Shakespearean critics. He remained involved with politics and religious ideology throughout his life, and his has been called one of the liveliest minds of the time.

But as his prose work expanded to become some of the finest examples of English literature, his addiction and depression worsened, and in 1813 he nearly died of an overdose. In 1816 he moved to the house of Dr James Gillman in Highgate, where he remained for the rest of his life. In May of that same year, *Christabel and Other Poems* was published, and his collected works appeared under the title *Sibylline Leaves* a year later.

For the last years of his life he became the 'Sage of Highgate', a talker of great renown and an essential member of the nineteenth-century intelligentsia. He was often visited by Sara Hutchinson, and by his wife and daughter, and he was able, in 1828, to tour Germany one last time with Wordsworth. His last book, *On the Constitution of Church and State*, was published in 1830, and it encompassed the newly coined concept of 'Clerisy', which named the cultivated among the professional classes as the vital element of a nation.

Coleridge died of a heart attack in Highgate on 25 July 1834.

Author's Note

Thomas Carlyle called Coleridge 'the king of men', and his poetry is as regal as its creator. He published a great deal throughout his lifetime, but his greatest works number few, for the eternal opium and his deep depressions nearly suffocated his keen mind, his unique vision. The following represent some of his greatest works and are emblematic of his fiery genius; his words drip with haunting imagery, and yet they are both perceptive and an unlikely combination of the profoundly political, the philosophical, and the supremely beautiful poetry of nature.

Chronology

1772	Samuel Taylor Coleridge born 21 October.
1781	Death of Coleridge's father.
1788	Elected Grecian.
1791	Attends Jesus College, Cambridge.
1792	Wins Browne medal for *Ode on the Slave Trade*.
1794	Begins *Religious Musings*. Tours Wales. Meets Robert Southey and plans pantisocracy.
1795	Begins poetical lectures. Marries Sara Fricker.
1796	Son, Hartley Coleridge, born. Writes for *The Watchman* and *Poems on Various Subjects*.
1797	Begins *Ancient Mariner*. Writes *Kubla Khan*. Walks with Wordsworths.
1798	Writes *Frost at Midnight*, *France: An Ode*. Meets Sara Hutchinson. Writes and reports for *Morning Post*.
1801	*Lyrical Ballads* published.
1802	Writes *Dejection: An Ode*. Sara Coleridge born.
1804	Appointed under-secretary to British High Commissioner in Malta.
1807	Hears Wordsworth read the *Prelude*.
1809	*The Friend* published.
1810	Quarrels with Wordsworth.
1812	Becomes ill.
1816	*Christabel*, *Kubla Khan* and *The Pains of Sleep* published. Accepted as a patient of James Gillman.
1817	*Biographia Literaria*, *Sibylline Leaves* and *Zapolya* published.
1818	Lectures on literary subjects. Meets Keats.
1828	Tours Netherlands and Germany with Wordsworths. *Poetical Works* published.
1830	*The Devil's Walk* reissued; Coleridge acknowledged.
1834	Dies 25 July, at Highgate.

To the Autumnal Moon

MILD SPLENDOUR of the various-vested Night!
Mother of wildly-working visions! hail!
I watch thy gliding, while with watery light
Thy weak eye glimmers through a fleecy veil;
And when thou lovest thy pale orb to shroud
Behind the gather'd blackness lost on high;
And when thou dartest from the wind-rent cloud
Thy placid lightning o'er the awaken'd sky.

Ah such is Hope as changeful and as fair!
Now dimly peering on the wistful sight;
Now hid behind the dragon-wing'd Despair:
But soon emerging in her radiant might
She o'er the sorrow-clouded breast of Care
Sails, like a meteor kindling in its flight.

Youth and Age

VERSE, A breeze mid blossoms straying,
Where Hope clung feeding, like a bee —
Both were mine! Life went a-maying
 With Nature, Hope, and Poesy,
  When I was young!

When I was young? — Ah, woful When!
Ah! for the change 'twixt Now and Then!
This breathing house not built with hands,
This body that does me grievous wrong,
 O'er aery cliffs and glittering sands,
 How lightly then it flashed along: —
Like those trim skiffs, unknown of yore,
 On winding lakes and rivers wide,
 That ask no aid of sail or oar,
That fear no spite of wind or tide!
Nought cared this body for wind or weather
When Youth and I lived in't together.

Flowers are lovely; Love is flower-like;
 Friendship is a sheltering tree;
O! the joys, that came down shower-like,
 Of Friendship, Love, and Liberty,
  Ere I was old!

Ere I was old? Ah woful Ere,
Which tells me, Youth's no longer here!
O Youth! for years so many and sweet,
'Tis known, that Thou and I were one,
 I'll think it but a fond conceit —
 It cannot be that Thou art gone!

Thy vesper-bell hath not yet toll'd: —
And thou wert aye a masker bold!
What strange disguise hast now put on,
To make believe, that thou art gone?
I see these locks in silvery slips,
This drooping gait, this altered size:
But Spring-tide blossoms on thy lips,
And tears take sunshine from thine eyes!
Life is but thought; so think I will
That Youth and I are house-mates still.

Dew-drops are the gems of morning,
But the tears of mournful eve!
Where no hope is, life's a warning
That only serves to make us grieve,
When we are old:

That only serves to make us grieve
With oft and tedious taking-leave,
Like some poor nigh-related guest,
That may not rudely be dismist;
Yet hath outstay'd his welcome while,
And tells the jest without the smile.

COLERIDGE

To the Nightingale

SISTER OF love-lorn Poets, Philomel!
How many Bards in city garret pent,
While at their window they with downward eye
Mark the faint Lamp-beam on the kennell'd mud,
And listen to the drowsy cry of Watchmen,
(Those hoarse unfeather'd Nightingales of Time!),
How many wretched Bards address thy name,
And Hers, the full-orb'd Queen that shines above.
But I *do* hear thee, and the high bough mark,
Within whose mild moon-mellow'd foliage hid
Though warblest sad thy pity-pleading strains.
O! have I listen'd, till my working soul,
Wak'd by those strains to thousand phantasies,
Absorb'd hath ceas'd to listen! Therefore oft,
I hymn thy name: and with a proud delight
Oft will I tell thee, MINSTREL of the MOON!
'Most musical, most melancholy' Bird!
That all thy soft diversities of tone,
Tho' sweeter far than the delicious airs
That vibrate from a white-arm's Lady's harp,
What time the languishment of lonely love
Melts in her eye, and heaves her breast of snow,
Are not so sweet, as is the love of her,
My SARA – best belov'd of human Kind!
When breathing the pure soul of Tenderness,
She thrills me with the HUSBAND's promised name!

LYRICAL ROMANTIC

Pain

ONCE COULD the Morn's first beams, the healthful breeze,
　　All Nature charm, and gay was every hour: —
　　But ah! not Music's self, nor fragrant bower
　　Can glad the trembling sense of wan Disease.
　　Now that the frequent pangs my frame assail,
　　Now that my sleepless eyes are sunk and dim,
　And seas of Pain seem waving through each limb —
　　Ah what can all Life's gilded scenes avail?
　I view the crowd, whom Youth and Health inspire,
　　Hear the loud laugh, and catch the sportive lay,
　　Then sigh and think — I too could laugh and play
　　And gaily sport it on the Muse's lyre,
　　Ere Tyrant Pain had chas'd away delight,
Ere the wild pulse throbb'd anguish thro' the night!

COLERIDGE

This Lime-Tree Bower My Prison

WELL, THEY are gone, and here must I remain,
This lime-tree bower my prison! I have lost
Beauties and feelings, such as would have been
Most sweet to my remembrance even when age
Had dimm'd mine eyes to blindness! They, meanwhile,
Friends, whom I never more may meet again,
On springy heath, along the hill-top edge,
Wander in gladness, and wind down, perchance,
To that still roaring dell, of which I told;
The roaring dell, o'erwooded, narrow, deep,
And only speckled by the mid-day sun;
Where its slim trunk the ash from rock to rock
Flings arching like a bridge; – that branchless ash,
Unsunn'd and damp, whose few poor yellow leaves
Ne'er tremble in the gale, yet tremble still,
Fann'd by the water-fall! and there my friends
Behold the dark green file of long lank weeds,
That all at once (a most fantastic sight!)
Still nod and drip beneath the dripping edge
Of the blue clay-stone.

Now, my friends emerge
Beneath the wide wide Heaven – and view again
The many-steepled tract magnificent
Of hilly fields and meadows, and the sea,
With some fair bark, perhaps, whose sails light up
The slip of smooth clear blue betwixt two Isles

Of purple shadow! Yes! they wander on
In gladness all; but thou, methinks, most glad,
My gentle-hearted Charles! for thou hast pined
And hunger'd after Nature, many a year,
In the great City pent, winning thy way
With sad yet patient soul, through evil and pain
And strange calamity! Ah! slowly sink
Behind the western ridge, thou glorious Sun!
Shine in the slant beams of the sinking orb,
Ye purple heath-flowers! richlier burn, ye clouds!
Live in the yellow light, ye distant groves!
And kindle, thou blue Ocean! So my friend
Struck with deep joy may stand, as I have stood,
Silent with swimming sense; yea, gazing till all doth seem
Less gross than bodily; and of such hues
As veil the Almighty Spirit, when yet he makes
Spirits perceive his presence.

A delight
Comes sudden on my heart, and I am glad
As I myself were there! Nor in this bower,
This little lime-tree bower, have I not mark'd
Much that has sooth'd me. Pale beneath the blaze
Hung the transparent foliage; and I watch'd
Some broad and sunny leaf, and lov'd to see
The shadow of the leaf and stem above
Dappling its sunshine! And that walnut-tree
Was richly ting'd, and a deep radiance lay
Full on the ancient ivy, which usurps
Those fronting elms, and now, with blackest mass
Makes their dark branches gleam a lighter hue
Through the late twilight: and though now the bat
Wheels silent by, and not a swallow twitters,
Yet still the solitary humble-bee
Sings in the bean-flower! Henceforth I shall know

That Nature ne'er deserts the wise and pure;
   No plot so narrow, be but Nature there,
   No waste so vacant, but may well employ
   Each faculty of sense, and keep the heart
   Awake to Love and Beauty! and sometimes
   'Tis well to be bereft of promis'd good,
   That we may lift the soul, and contemplate
   With lively joy the joys we cannot share.
My gentle-hearted Charles! When the last rook
   Beat its straight path along the dusky air
Homewards, I blest it! deeming its black wing
   (Now a dim speck, now vanishing in light)
   Had cross'd the mighty Orb's dilated glory,
While thou stood'st gazing; or, when all was still,
Flew creeking o'er thy head, and had a charm
For thee, my gentle-hearted Charles, to whom
   No sound is dissonant which tells of Life.

The Rime of the Ancient Mariner

Part I

IT IS an ancient Mariner,
And he stoppeth one of three.
"By thy long grey beard and glittering eye,
Now wherefore stopp'st thou me?

The Bridegroom's doors are opened wide,
And I am next of kin;
The guests are met, the feast is set:
May'st hear the merry din."

He holds him with his skinny hand,
"There was a ship," quoth he.
"Hold off! unhand me, grey-beard loon!"
Eftsoons his hand dropt he.

He holds him with his glittering eye –
The Wedding-Guest stood still,
And listens like a three years' child:
The Mariner hath his will.
The Wedding-Guest sat on a stone:
He cannot choose but hear;
And thus spake on that ancient man,
The bright-eyed Mariner.

"The ship was cheered, the harbour cleared,
Merrily did we drop
Below the kirk, below the hill,
Below the lighthouse top.
The Sun came up upon the left,
Out of the sea came he!
And he shone bright, and on the right
Went down into the sea.

Higher and higher every day,
Till over the mast at noon –"
The Wedding-Guest here beat his breast,
For he heard the loud bassoon.

The bride hath paced into the hall,
Red as a rose is she;
Nodding their heads before her goes
The merry minstrelsy.

The Wedding-Guest he beat his breast,
Yet he cannot choose but hear;
And thus spake on that ancient man,
The bright-eyed Mariner.

"And now the STORM-BLAST came, and he
  Was tyrannous and strong;
He struck with his o'ertaking wings,
  And chased us south along.

With sloping masts and dripping prow,
  As who pursued with yell and blow
Still treads the shadow of his foe,
  And forward bends his head,
The ship drove fast, loud roared the blast,
  And southward aye we fled.

And now there came both mist and snow,
  And it grew wondrous cold:
And ice, mast-high, came floating by,
  As green as emerald.

And through the drifts the snowy clifts
  Did send a dismal sheen:
Nor shapes of men nor beasts we ken –
  The ice was all between.

The ice was here, the ice was there,
  The ice was all around:
It cracked and growled, and roared and howled,
  Like noises in a swound!

At length did cross an Albatross,
  Through the fog it came;
As if it had been a Christian soul,
  We hailed it in God's name.

It ate the food it ne'er had eat,
And round and round it flew.
The ice did split with a thunder-fit;
The helmsman steered us through!

And a good south wind sprung up behind;
The Albatross did follow,
And every day, for food or play,
Came to the mariners' hollo!

In mist or cloud, on mast or shroud,
It perched for vespers nine;
Whiles all the night, through fog-smoke white,
Glimmered the white Moon-shine."

"God save thee, ancient Mariner!
From the fiends, that plague thee thus! –
Why look'st thou so?" – "With my cross-bow
I shot the ALBATROSS."

Part II

The Sun now upon the right:
Out of the sea came he,
Still hid in mist, and on the left
Went down into the sea.

And the good south wind still blew behind,
But no sweet bird did follow,
Nor any day for food or play
Came to the mariners' hollo!

And I had done a hellish thing,
And it would work 'em woe:
For all averred, I had killed the bird
That made the breeze to blow.
Ah wretch! said they, the bird to slay,
That made the breeze to blow!

Nor dim nor red, like God's own head,
The glorious Sun uprist:
Then all averred, I had killed the bird
That brought the fog and mist.
'Twas right, said they, such birds to slay,
That bring the fog and mist.

The fair breeze blew, the white foam flew,
The furrow followed free;
We were the first that ever burst
Into that silent sea.
Down dropt the breeze, the sails dropt down,
'Twas sad as sad could be;
And we did speak only to break
The silence of the sea!

All in a hot and copper sky,
The bloody Sun, at noon,
Right up above the mast did stand,
No bigger than the Moon.

Day after day, day after day,
We stuck, nor breath nor motion;
As idle as a painted ship
Upon a painted ocean.

Water, water, every where,
And all the boards did shrink;
Water, water, every where,
Nor any drop to drink.

The very deep did rot: O Christ!
That ever this should be!
Yea, slimy things did crawl with legs
Upon the slimy sea.
About, about, in reel and rout
The death-fires danced at night;
The water, like a witch's oils,
Burnt green, and blue and white.

And some in dreams assuréd were
Of the Spirit that plagued us so;
Nine fathom deep he had followed us
From the land of mist and snow.

And every tongue, through utter drought,
Was withered at the root;
We could not speak, no more than if
We had been choked with soot.

Ah! well a-day! what evil looks
Had I from old and young!
Instead of the cross, the Albatross
About my neck was hung.

Part III

There passed a weary time. Each throat
Was parched, and glazed each eye.
A weary time! a weary time!
How glazed each weary eye,
When looking westward, I beheld
A something in the sky.

At first it seemed a little speck,
And then it seemed a mist;
It moved and moved, and took at last
A certain shape, I wist.

A speck, a mist, a shape, I wist!
And still it neared and neared:
As if it dodged a water-sprite,
It plunged and tacked and veered.

With throats unslaked, with black lips baked,
We could nor laugh nor wail;
Through utter drought all dumb we stood!
I bit my arm, I sucked the blood,
And cried, A sail! a sail!

With throats unslaked, with black lips baked,
Agape they heard me call:
Gramercy! they for joy did grin,
And all at once their breath drew in,
As they were drinking all.

See! see! (I cried) she tacks no more!
Hither to work us weal;
Without a breeze, without a tide,
She steadies with upright keel!

The western wave was all a-flame.
The day was well nigh done!
Almost upon the western wave
Rested the broad bright Sun;
When that strange shape drove suddenly
Betwixt us and the Sun.

And straight the Sun was flecked with bars,
(Heaven's Mother send us grace!)
As if through a dungeon-grate he peered
With broad and burning face.

Alas! (thought I, and my heart beat loud)
How fast she nears and nears!
Are those *her* sails that glance in the Sun,
Like restless gossameres?

Are those *her* ribs through which the Sun
Did peer, as through a grate?
And is that Woman all her crew?
Is that a DEATH? and are there two?
Is DEATH that woman's mate?

Her lips were red, *her* looks were free,
Her locks were yellow as gold:
Her skin was as white as leprosy,
The Night-mare LIFE-IN-DEATH was she,
Who thicks man's blood with cold.

The naked hulk alongside came,
And the twain were casting dice;
'The game is done! I've won! I've won!'
Quoth she, and whistles thrice.

The Sun's rim dips; the stars rush out:
At one stride comes the dark;
With far-heard whisper, o'er the sea,
Off shot the spectre-bark.

We listened and looked sideways up!
Fear at my heart, as at a cup,
My life-blood seemed to sip!
The stars were dim, and thick the night,
The steersman's face by his lamp gleamed white;

From the sails the dew did drip –
Till clomb above the eastern bar
The hornéd Moon, with one bright star
Within the nether tip.

One after one, by the star-dogged Moon,
Too quick for groan or sigh,
Each turned his face with ghastly pang,
And cursed me with his eye.

Four times fifty living men,
(And I heard not sigh nor groan)
With heavy thump, a lifeless lump,
They dropped down one by one.
The souls did from their bodies fly, –
They fled to bliss or woe!
And every soul, it passed me by,
Like the whizz of my cross-bow!"

Part IV

"I fear thee, ancient Mariner!
I fear thy skinny hand!
And thou art long, and lank, and brown,
As is the ribbed sea-sand.

I fear thee and thy glittering eye,
And thy skinny hand, so brown." –
"Fear not, fear not, thou Wedding-Guest!
This body dropt not down.

Alone, alone, all, all alone,
Alone on a wide wide sea!
And never a saint took pity on
My soul in agony.

The many men, so beautiful!
And they all dead did lie:
And a thousand thousand slimy things
Lived on; and so did I.

I looked upon the rotting sea,
And drew my eyes away;
I looked upon the rotting deck,
And there the dead men lay

I looked to heaven, and tried to pray;
But or ever a prayer had gusht,
A wicked whisper came, and made
My heart as dry as dust.
I closed my lids, and kept them close,
And the balls like pulses beat;
For the sky and the sea, and the sea and the sky
Lay like a load on my weary eye,

LYRICAL ROMANTIC

And the dead were at my feet.
The cold sweat melted from their limbs,
Nor rot nor reek did they:
The look with which they looked on me
Had never passed away.

An orphan's curse would drag to hell
A spirit from on high;
But oh! more horrible than that
Is the curse in a dead man's eye!
Seven days, seven nights, I saw that curse,
And yet I could not die.

The moving Moon went up the sky,
And no where did abide:
Softly she was going up,
And a star or two beside –

Her beams bemocked the sultry main,
Like April hoar-frost spread;
But where the ship's huge shadow lay,
The charmèd water burnt alway
A still and awful red.

Beyond the shadow of the ship,
I watched the water-snakes:
They moved in tracks of shining white,
And when they reared, the elfish light
Fell off in hoary flakes.

Within the shadow of the ship
I watched their rich attire:
Blue, glossy green, and velvet black,
They coiled and swam; and every track
Was a flash of golden fire.

O happy living things! no tongue
Their beauty might declare:
A spring of love gushed from my heart,
And I blessed them unaware:
Sure my kind saint took pity on me,
And I blessed them unaware.

The self-same moment I could pray;
And from my neck so free
The Albatross fell off, and sank
Like lead into the sea.

Part V

Oh sleep! it is a gentle thing,
Beloved from pole to pole!
To Mary Queen the praise be given!
She sent the gentle sleep from Heaven,
That slid into my soul.

The silly buckets on the deck,
That had so long remained,
I dreamt that they were filled with dew;
And when I awoke, it rained.

My lips were wet, my throat was cold,
My garments all were dank;
Sure I had drunken in my dreams,
And still my body drank.
I moved, and could not feel my limbs:
I was so light – almost
I thought that I had died in sleep,
And was a blesséd ghost.

COLERIDGE

And soon I heard a roaring wind:
It did not come anear;
But with its sound it shook the sails,
That were so thin and sere.

The upper air burst into life!
And a hundred fire-flags sheen,
To and fro they were hurried about!
And to and fro, and in and out,
The wan stars danced between.

And the coming wind did roar more loud,
And the sails did sigh like sedge;
And the rain poured down from one black cloud;
The Moon was at its edge.

LYRICAL ROMANTIC

>The thick black cloud was cleft, and still
>   The Moon was at its side:
>Like waters shot from some high crag,
>The lightning fell with never a jag,
>   A river steep and wide.
>
>The loud wind never reached the ship,
>   Yet now the ship moved on!
>Beneath the lightning and the Moon
>   The dead men gave a groan.
>They groaned, they stirred, they all uprose,
>   Nor spake, nor moved their eyes;
>It had been strange, even in a dream,
>   To have seen those dead men rise.
>The helmsman steered, the ship moved on;

Yet never a breeze up-blew;
The mariners all 'gan work the ropes,
Where they were wont to do;
They raised their limbs like lifeless tools –
We were a ghastly crew.

The body of my brother's son
Stood by me, knee to knee:
The body and I pulled at one rope,
But he said nought to me."
"I fear thee, ancient Mariner!"
"Be calm, thou Wedding-Guest!
'Twas not those souls that fled in pain,
Which to their corses came again,
But a troop of spirits blest:

For when it dawned – they dropped their arms,
And clustered round the mast;
Sweet sounds rose slowly through their mouths,
And from their bodies passed.

Around, around, flew each sweet sound,
Then darted to the Sun;
Slowly the sounds came back again,
Now mixed, now one by one.

Sometimes a-dropping from the sky
I heard the sky-lark sing;
Sometimes all little birds that are,
How they seemed to fill the sea and air
With their sweet jargoning!

And now 'twas like all instruments,
  Now like a lonely flute;
And now it is an angel's song,
  That makes the heavens be mute.

It ceased; yet still the sails made on
  A pleasant noise till noon,
  A noise like of a hidden brook
  In the leafy month of June,
That to the sleeping woods all night
  Singeth a quiet tune.

Till noon we quietly sailed on,
  Yet never a breeze did breathe:
Slowly and smoothly went the ship,
  Moved onward from beneath.

Under the keel nine fathom deep,
  From the land of mist and snow,
  The spirit slid: and it was he
  That made the ship to go.
The sails at noon left off their tune,
  And the ship stood still also.

The Sun, right up above the mast,
  Had fixed her to the ocean:
  But in a minute she 'gan stir,
  With a short uneasy motion –
Backwards and forwards half her length
  With a short uneasy motion.

Then like a pawing horse let go,
She made a sudden bound:
It flung the blood into my head,
And I fell down in a swound.
How long in that same fit I lay,
I have not to declare;
But ere my living life returned,
I heard and in my soul discerned
Two voices in the air.

'Is it he?' quoth one, 'Is this the man?
By him who died on cross,
With his cruel bow he laid full low
The harmless Albatross.

The spirit who bideth by himself
In the land of mist and snow,
He loved the bird that loved the man
Who shot him with his bow.'

The other was a softer voice,
As soft as honey-dew:
Quoth he, "The man hath penance done,
And penance more will do.'

Part VI

FIRST VOICE
'But tell me, tell me! speak again,
Thy soft response renewing –
What makes that ship drive on so fast?
What is the ocean doing?'

LYRICAL ROMANTIC

SECOND VOICE
'Still as a slave before his lord,
The ocean hath no blast;
His great bright eye most silently
Up to the Moon is cast —

If he may know which way to go;
For she guides him smooth or grim.
See, brother, see! how graciously
She looketh down on him.'

FIRST VOICE
'But why drives on that ship so fast,
Without or wave or wind?'

SECOND VOICE
'The air is cut away before,
And closes from behind.

Fly, brother, fly! more high, more high!
Or we shall be belated:
For slow and slow that ship will go,
When the Mariner's trance is abated.'

I woke, and we were sailing on
As in a gentle weather:
'Twas night, calm night, the moon was high;
The dead men stood together.

All stood together on the deck,
For a charnel-dungeon fitter:
All fixed on me their stony eyes,
That in the Moon did glitter.

The pang, the curse, with which they died,
    Had never passed away:
I could not draw my eyes from theirs,
    Nor turn them up to pray.

And now this spell was snapt: once more
    I viewed the ocean green,
And looked far forth, yet little saw
    Of what had else been seen –

Like one, that on a lonesome road
    Doth walk in fear and dread,
And having once turned round walks on,
    And turns no more his head;
Because he knows, a frightful fiend
    Doth close behind him tread.
But soon there breathed a wind on me,
    Nor sound nor motion made:
Its path was not upon the sea,
    In ripple or in shade.

It raised my hair, it fanned my cheek
    Like a meadow-gale of spring –
It mingled strangely with my fears,
    Yet it felt like a welcoming.

Swiftly, swiftly flew the ship,
    Yet she sailed softly too:
Sweetly, sweetly blew the breeze –
    On me alone it blew.

Oh! dream of joy! is this indeed
    The light-house top I see?
Is this the hill? is this the kirk?
    Is this mine own countree?

We drifted o'er the harbour-bar,
And I with sobs did pray –
O let me be awake, my God!
Or let me sleep alway.
The harbour-bay was clear as glass,
So smoothy it was strewn!
And on the bay the moonlight lay,
And the shadow of the Moon.

The rock shone bright, the kirk no less,
That stands above the rock:
The moonlight steeped in silentness
The steady weathercock.

And the bay was white with silent light,
Till rising from the same,
Full many shapes, that shadows were,
In crimson colours came.

A little distance from the prow
Those crimson shadows were:
I turned my eyes upon the deck –
Oh, Christ! what saw I there!

Each corse lay flat, lifeless and flat,
And, by the holy rood!
A man all light, a seraph-man,
On every corse there stood.

This seraph-band, each waved his hand:
It was a heavenly sight!
They stood as signals to the land,
Each one a lovely light;

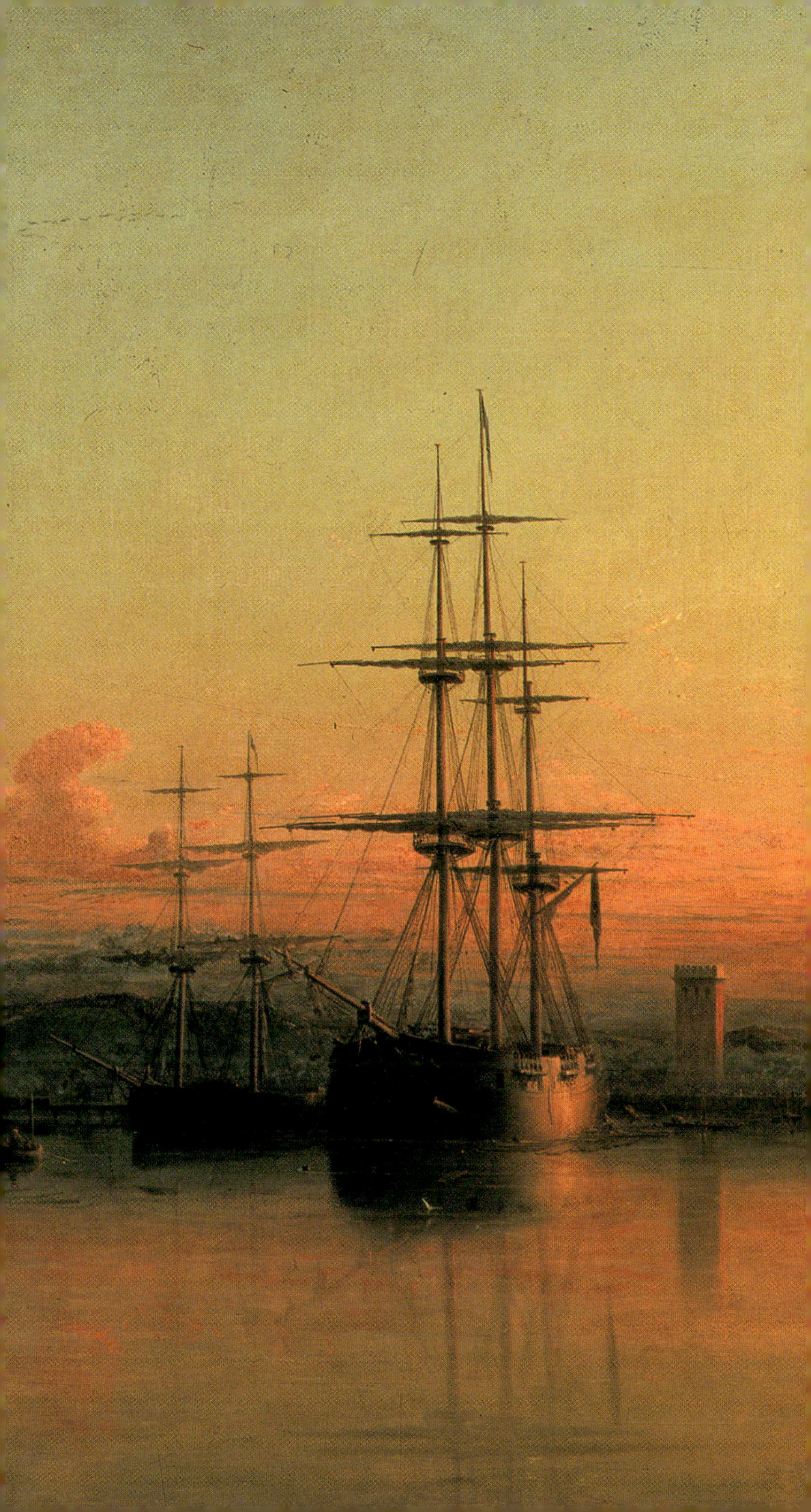

This seraph-band, each waved his hand,
No voice did they impart –
No voice; but oh! the silence sank
Like music on my heart.

But soon I heard the dash of oars,
I heard the Pilot's cheer;
My head was turned perforce away
And I saw a boat appear.

The Pilot and the Pilot's boy,
I heard them coming fast:
Dear Lord in Heaven! it was a joy
The dead men could not blast.

I saw a third – I heard his voice:
It is the Hermit good!
He singeth loud his godly hymns
That he makes in the wood.
He'll shrieve my soul, he'll wash away
The Albatross's blood.

Part VII

This Hermit good lives in that wood
Which slopes down to the sea.
How loudly his sweet voice he rears!
He loves to talk with marineres
That come from a far countree.

He kneels at morn, and noon, and eve –
He hath a cushion plump:
It is the moss that wholly hides
The rotted old oak-stump.

The skiff-boat neared: I heard them talk,
    'Why, this is strange, I trow!
Where are those lights so many and fair,
    That signal made but now?'

'Strange, by my faith!' the Hermit said –
    'And they answered not our cheer!
The planks looked warped! and see those sails,
    How thin they are and sere!
I never saw aught like to them,
    Unless perchance it were
Brown skeletons of leaves that lag
    My forest-brook along;
When the ivy-tod is heavy with snow,
And the owlet whoops to the wolf below,
    That eats the she-wolf's young.'
'Dear Lord! it hath a fiendish look –
    (The Pilot made reply)
I am a-feared' – 'Push on, push on!'
    Said the Hermit cheerily.

The boat came closer to the ship,
    But I nor spake nor stirred;
The boat came close beneath the ship,
    And straight a sound was heard.

Under the water it rumbled on,
    Still louder and more dread:
It reached the ship, it split the bay;
    The ship went down like lead.

Stunned by that loud and dreadful sound,
Which sky and ocean smote,
Like one that hath been seven days drowned
My body lay afloat;
But swift as dreams, myself I found
Within the Pilot's boat:

Upon the whirl, where sank the ship,
The boat spun round and round;
And all was still, save that the hill
Was telling of the sound.

I moved my lips – the Pilot shrieked
And fell down in a fit;
The holy Hermit raised his eyes,
And prayed where he did sit.

I took the oars: the Pilot's boy,
Who now doth crazy go,
Laughed loud and long, and all the while
His eyes went to and fro.
'Ha! ha!' quoth he, 'full plain I see,
The Devil knows how to row.'

And now, all in my own countree,
I stood on the firm land!
The Hermit stepped forth from the boat,
And scarely he could stand.

'O shrieve me, shrieve me, holy man!'
The Hermit crossed his brow.
'Say quick,' quoth he, 'I bid thee say –
What manner of man art thou?'

Fortwith this frame of mine was wrenched
With a woful agony,
Which forced me to begin my tale;
And then it left me free.

Since then, at an uncertain hour,
That agony returns:
And till my ghastly tale is told,
This heart within me burns.
I pass, like night, from land to land;
I have strange power of speech;
That moment that his face I see,
I know the man that must hear me:
To him my tale I teach.

What loud uproar bursts from that door!
The wedding-guests are there:
But in the garden-bower the bride
And bride-maids singing are:
And hark the little vesper bell,
Which biddeth me to prayer!

O Wedding-Guest! this soul hath been
Alone on a wide wide sea:
So lonely 'twas, that God himself
Scarce seeméd there to be.

O sweeter than the marriage-feast,
'Tis sweeter far to me,
To walk together to the kirk
With a goodly company! —

COLERIDGE

54

To walk together to the kirk,
    And all together pray,
While each to his great Father bends,
Old men, and babes, and loving friends
    And youths and maidens gay!

Farewell, farewell! but this I tell
    To thee, thou Wedding-Guest!
He prayeth well, who loveth well
    Both man and bird and beast.

He prayeth best, who loveth best
    All things both great and small;
For the dear God who loveth us,
    He made and loveth all."

The Mariner, whose eye is bright,
    Whose beard with age is hoar,
Is gone: and now the Wedding-Guest
Turned from the bridegroom's door.
He went like one that hath been stunned,
    And is of sense forlorn:
A sadder and a wiser man,
He rose the morrow morn.

COLERIDGE

Kubla Khan

IN XANADU did Kubla Khan
A stately pleasure-dome decree:
Where Alph, the sacred river, ran
Through caverns measureless to man
Down to a sunless sea.
So twice five miles of fertile ground
With walls and towers were girdled round:
And there were gardens bright with sinuous rills,
Where blossomed many an incense-bearing tree;
And here were forests ancient as the hills,
Enfolding sunny spots of greenery.

But oh! that deep romantic chasm which slanted
Down the green hill athwart a cedarn cover!
A savage place! as holy and enchanted
As e'er beneath a waning moon was haunted
By woman wailing for her demon-lover!
And from this chasm, with ceaseless turmoil seething.
As if this earth in fast thick pants were breathing,
A mighty fountain momently was forced:
Amid whose swift half-intermitted burst
Huge fragments vaulted like rebounding hail,
Or chaffy grain beneath the thresher's flail:
And 'mid these dancing rocks at once and ever
It flung up momently the sacred river,
Five miles meandering with a mazy motion
Through wood and dale the sacred river ran,
Then reached the caverns measureless to man,
And sank in tumult to a lifeless ocean:
And 'mid this tumult Kubla heard from far
Ancestral voices prophesying war!

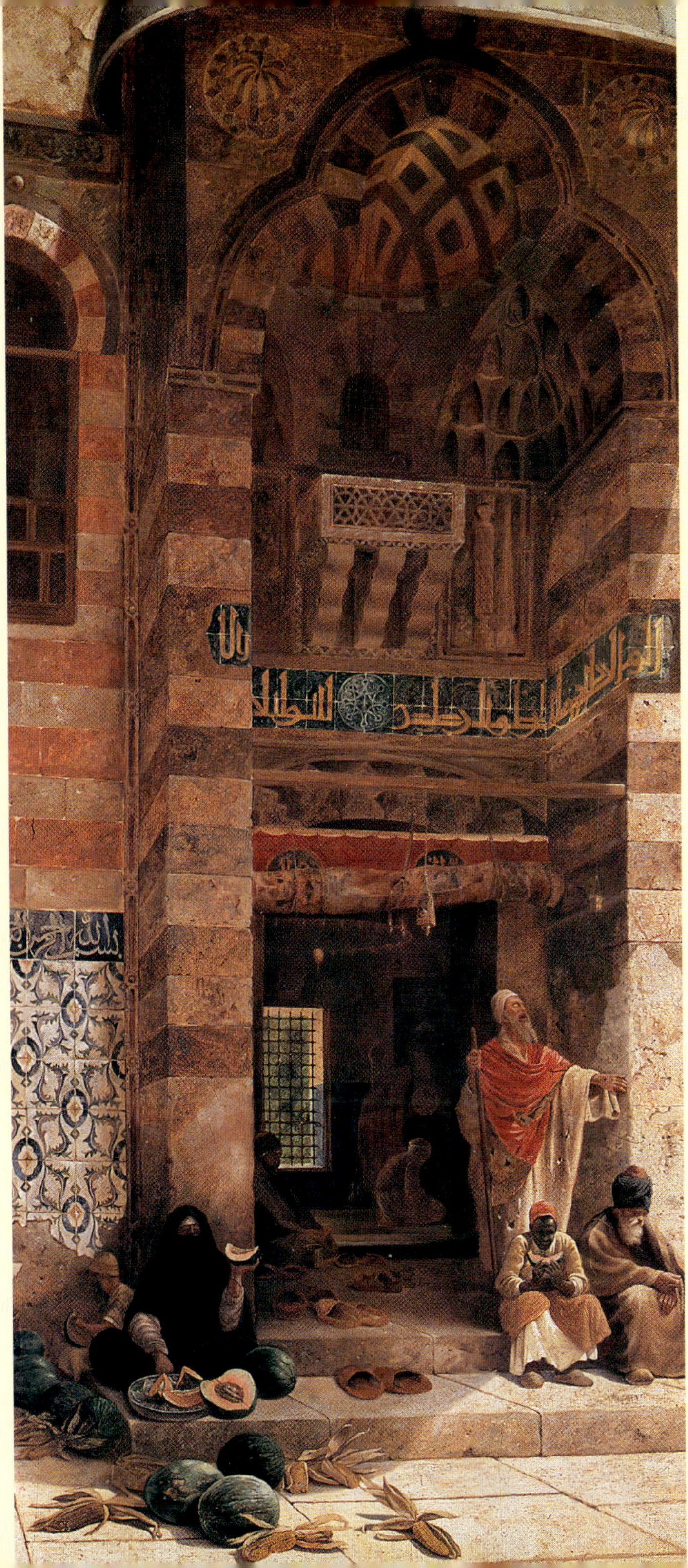

The shadow of the dome of pleasure
Floated midway on the waves;
Where was heard the mingled measure
From the fountain and the caves.
It was a miracle of rare device,
A sunny pleasure-dome with caves of ice!

A damsel with a dulcimer
In a vision once I saw:
It was an Abyssinian maid,
And on her dulcimer she played,
Singing of Mount Abora.
Could I revive within me
Her symphony and song,
To such a deep delight 'twould win me,
That with music loud and long,
I would build that dome in air,
That sunny dome! those caves of ice!
And all who heard should see them there,
And all should cry, Beware! Beware!
His flashing eyes, his floating hair!
Weave a circle round him thrice,
And close your eyes with holy dread,
For he on honey-dew hath fed,
And drunk the milk of Paradise.

LYRICAL ROMANTIC

The Exchange

WE PLEDGED our hearts, my love and I, –
I in my arms the maiden clasping;
I could not guess the reason why,
But, oh! I trembled like an aspen.

Her father's love she bade me gain;
I went, but shook like any reed!
I strove to act the man – in vain!
We had exchanged our hearts indeed.

Frost at Midnight

THE FROST performs its secret ministry,
Unhelped by any wind. The owlet's cry
Came loud – and hark, again! loud as before.
The inmates of my cottage, all at rest,
Have left me to that solitude, which suits
Abstruser musings: save that at my side
My cradled infant slumbers peacefully.
'Tis calm indeed! so calm, that it disturbs
And vexes meditation with its strange
And extreme silentness. Sea, hill, and wood,
With all the numberless goings-on of life,
Inaudible as dreams! the thin blue flame
Lies on my low-burnt fire, and quivers not;
Only that film, which fluttered on the grate,
Still flutters there, the sole unquiet thing.
Methinks, its motion in this hush of nature
Gives it dim sympathies with me who live,
Making it a companionable form,
Whose puny flaps and freaks the idling Spirit
By its own moods interprets, every where
Echo or mirror seeking of itself,
And makes a toy of Thought.

But O! how oft,
How oft, at school, with most believing mind,
Presageful, have I gazed upon the bars,
To watch that fluttering stranger! and as oft
With unclosed lids, already had I dreamt
Of my sweet birth-place, and the old church-tower,
Whose bells, the poor man's only music, rang
From morn to evening, all the hot Fair-day,

LYRICAL ROMANTIC

So sweetly, that they stirred and haunted me
With a wild pleasure, falling on mine ear
Most like articulate sounds of things to come!
So gazed I, till the soothing things I dreamt,
Lulled me to sleep, and sleep prolonged my dreams!
And so I brooded all the following morn,
Awed by the stern preceptor's face, mine eye
Fixed with mock study on my swimming book:
Save if the door half opened, and I snatched
A hasty glance, and still my heart leaped up,
For still I hoped to see the stranger's face,
Townsman, or aunt, or sister more beloved,
My play-mate when we both were clothed alike!

Dear Babe, that sleepest cradled by my side,
Whose gentle breathings, heard in this deep calm,
Fill up the interspersèd vacancies
And momentary pauses of the thought!
My babe so beautiful! it thrills my heart
With tender gladness, thus to look at thee,
And think that thou shalt learn far other lore,
And in far other scenes! For I was reared
In the great city, pent 'mid cloisters dim,
And saw nought lovely but the sky and stars.
But thou, my babe! shalt wander like a breeze
By lakes and sandy shores, beneath the crags
Of ancient mountain, and beneath the clouds,
Which image in their bulk both lakes and shores
And mountain crags: so shalt thou see and hear
The lovely shapes and sounds intelligible
Of that eternal language, which thy God
Utters, who from eternity doth teach
Himself in all, and all things in himself.
Great universal Teacher! he shall mould
Thy spirit, and by giving make it ask.

Therefore all seasons shall be sweet to thee,
Whether the summer clothe the general earth
With greenness, or the redbreast sit and sing
Betwixt the tufts of snow on the bare branch
Of mossy apple-tree, while the nigh thatch
Smokes in the sun-thaw; whether the eave-drops fall
Heard only in the trances of the blast,
Or if the secret ministry of frost
Shall hang them up in silent icicles,
Quietly shining to the quiet Moon.

Song

THOUGH VEILED in spires of myrtle wreath,
Love is a sword that cuts its sheath,
And through the clefts, itself has made,
We spy the flashes of the blade!

But through the clefts, itself has made,
We likewise see Love's flashing blade
By rust consumed or snapt in twain:
And only hilt and stump remain.

Christabel
— EXTRACT —

Part 1

'TIS THE middle of night by the castle clock,
And the owls have awakened the crowing cock;
Tu – whit! – Tu – whoo!
And hark, again! the crowing cock,
How drowsily it crew.
Sir Leoline, the Baron rich,
Hath a toothless mastiff bitch;
From her kennel beneath the rock
She maketh answer to the clock,
Four for the quarters, and twelve for the hour;
Ever and aye, by shine and shower,
Sixteen short howls, not over loud;
Some say, she sees my lady's shroud.
Is the night chilly and dark?
The night is chilly, but not dark.
The thin gray cloud is spread on high,
It covers but not hides the sky.
The moon is behind, and at the full;
And yet she looks both small and dull.
The night is chill, the cloud is gray:
'Tis a month before the month of May,
And the Spring comes slowly up this way.

The lovely lady, Christabel,
Whom her father loves so well,
What makes her in the wood so late,
A furlong from the castle gate?
She had dreams all yesternight
Of her own betrothéd knight;
And she in the midnight wood will pray

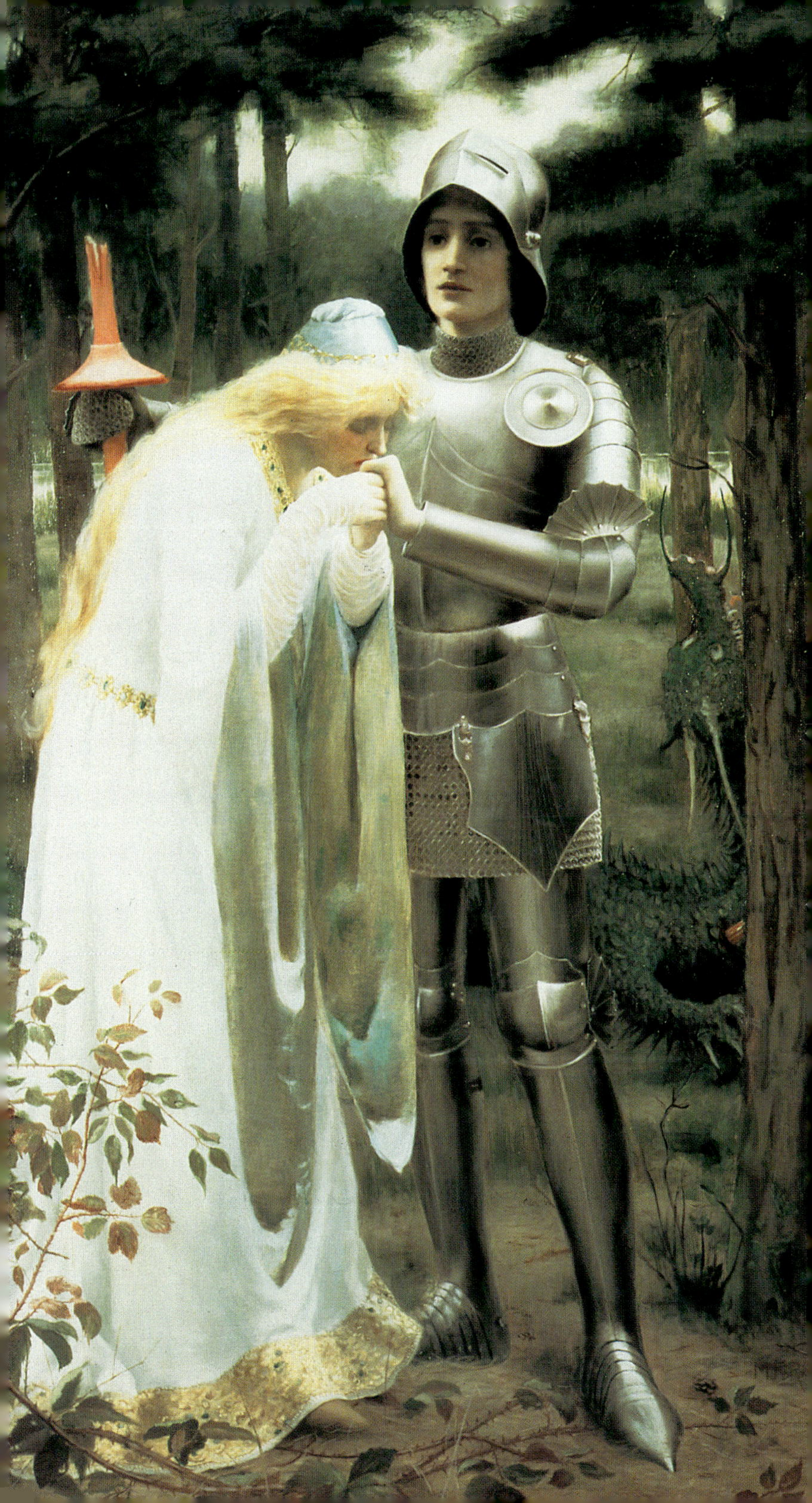

For the weal of her lover that's far away.
She stole along, she nothing spoke,
The sighs she heaved were soft and low,
And naught was green upon the oak
But moss and rarest misletoe:
She kneels beneath the huge oak tree,
And in silence prayeth she.

The lady sprang up suddenly,
The lovely lady, Christabel!
It moaned as near, as near can be,
But what it is she cannot tell.—
On the other side it seems to be,
Of the huge, broad-breasted, old oak tree.

The night is chill; the forest bare;
Is it the wind that moaneth bleak?
There is not wind enough in the air
To move away the ringlet curl
From the lovely lady's cheek—
There is not wind enough to twirl
The one red leaf, the last of its clan,
That dances as often as dance it can,
Hanging so light, and hanging so high,
On the topmost twig that looks up at the sky.

Hush, beating heart of Christabel!
Jesu, Maria, shield her well!
She folded her arms beneath her cloak,
And stole to the other side of the oak.
What sees she there?

There she sees a damsel bright,
Drest in a silken robe of white,
That shadowy in the moonlight shone:

The neck that made that white robe wan,
Her stately neck, and arms were bare;
Her blue-veined feet unsandal'd were,
And wildly glittered here and there
The gems entangled in her hair.
I guess, 'twas frightful there to see
A lady so richly clad as she –
Beautiful exceedingly!

Mary mother, save me now!
(Said Christabel,) And who art thou?

The lady strange made answer meet,
And her voice was faint and sweet: –
Have pity on my sore distress,
I scarce can speak for weariness:
Stretch forth thy hand, and have no fear!
Said Christabel, How camest thou here?
And the lady, whose voice was faint and sweet,
Did thus pursue her answer meet: –

My sire is of a noble line,
And my name is Geraldine:
Five warriors seized me yestermorn,
Me, even me, a maid forlorn:
They choked my cries with force and fright,
And tied me on a palfrey white.
The palfrey was as fleet as wind,
And they rode furiously behind.
They spurred amain, their steeds were white:
And once we crossed the shade of night.
As sure as Heaven shall rescue me,
I have no thought what men they be;
Nor do I know how long it is
(For I have lain entranced I wis)

Since one, the tallest of the five,
Took me from the palfrey's back,
A weary woman, scarce alive.
Some muttered words his comrades spoke:
He placed me underneath this oak;
He swore they would return with haste;
Whither they went I cannot tell—
I thought I heard, some minutes past,
Sounds as of a castle bell.
Stretch forth thy hand (thus ended she),
And help a wretched maid to flee.

Then Christabel stretched forth her hand,
And comforted fair Geraldine:
O well, bright dame! may you command
The service of Sir Leoline;
And gladly our stout chivalry
Will he send forth and friends withal
To guide and guard you safe and free
Home to your noble father's hall.

She rose: and forth with steps they passed
That strove to be, and were not, fast.
Her gracious stars the lady blest,
And thus spake on sweet Christabel:
All our household are at rest,
The hall as silent as the cell;
Sir Leoline is weak in health,
And may not well awakened be,
But we will move as if in stealth,
And I beseech your courtesy,
This night, to share your couch with me.

They crossed the moat, and Christabel
Took the key that fitted well;
A little door she opened straight,
All in the middle of the gate;
The gate that was ironed within and without,
Where an army in battle array had marched out.
The lady sank, belike through pain,
And Christabel with might and main
Lifted her up, a weary weight,
Over the threshold of the gate:
Then the lady rose again,
And moved, as she were not in pain.

So free from danger, free from fear,
They crossed the court: right glad they were.
And Christabel devoutly cried
To the lady by her side,
Praise we the Virgin all divine
Who hath rescued thee from thy distress!
Alas, alas! said Geraldine,
I cannot speak for weariness.
So free from danger, free from fear,
They crossed the court: right glad they were.

Outside her kennel, the mastiff old
Lay fast asleep, in moonshine cold.
The mastiff old did not awake,
Yet she an angry moan did make!
And what can ail the mastiff bitch?
Never till now she uttered yell
Beneath the eye of Christabel.
Perhaps it is the owlet's scritch:
For what can ail the mastiff bitch?

COLERIDGE

They passed the hall, that echoes still,
Pass as lightly as you will!
The brands were flat, the brands were dying,
Amid their own white ashes lying;
But when the lady passed, there came
A tongue of light, a fit of flame;
And Christabel saw the lady's eye,
And nothing else saw she thereby,
Save the boss of the shield of Sir Leoline tall,
Which hung in a murky old niche in the wall.
O softly tread, said Christabel,
My father seldom sleepeth well.

Sweet Christabel her feet doth bare,
And jealous of the listening air
They steal their way from stair to stair,
Now in glimmer, and now in gloom,
And now they pass the Baron's room,
As still as death, with stifled breath!
And now have reached her chamber door;
And now doth Geraldine press down
The rushes of the chamber floor.

The moon shines dim in the open air,
And not a moonbeam enters here.
But they without its light can see
The chamber carved so curiously,
Carved with figures strange and sweet,

All made out of the carver's brain,
For a lady's chamber meet:
The lamp with twofold silver chain
Is fastened to an angel's feet.

The silver lamp burns dead and dim;
But Christabel the lamp will trim.
She trimmed the lamp, and made it bright,
And left it swinging to and fro,
While Geraldine, in wretched plight,
Sank down upon the floor below.

O weary lady, Geraldine,
I pray you, drink this cordial wine!
It is a wine of virtuous powers;
My mother made it of wild flowers.

And will your mother pity me,
Who am a maiden most forlorn?
Christabel answered — Woe is me!
She died the hour that I was born.
I have heard the grey-haired friar tell
How on her death-bed she did say,
That she should hear the castle-bell
Strike twelve upon my wedding-day.
O mother dear! that thou wert here!

I would, said Geraldine, she were!
But soon with altered voice, said she –
"Off, wandering mother! Peak and pine!
I have power to bid thee flee."
Alas! what ails poor Geraldine?
Why stares she with unsettled eye?
Can she the bodiless dead espy?
And why with hollow voice cries she,
"Off, woman, off! this hour is mine –
Though thou her guardian spirit be,
Off, woman, off! 'tis given to me."

Then Christabel knelt by the lady's side,
And raised to heaven her eyes so blue —
 Alas! said she, this ghastly ride —
 Dear lady! it hath wildered you!
The lady wiped her moist cold brow,
And faintly said, "'tis over now!"

Again the wild-flower wine she drank:
Her fair large eyes 'gan glitter bright,
And from the floor whereon she sank,
 The lofty lady stood upright:
 She was most beautiful to see,
 Like a lady of a far countrée.

 And thus the lofty lady spake—
"All they who live in the upper sky,
 Do love you, holy Christabel!
And you love them, and for their sake
 And for the good which me befel,
 Even I in my degree will try,
 Fair maiden, to requite you well.
 But now unrobe yourself; for I
 Must pray, ere yet in bed I lie."
 Quoth Christabel, So let it be!
 And as the lady bade, did she.
 Her gentle limbs did she undress,
 And lay down in her loveliness.

But through her brain of weal and woe
So many thoughts moved to and fro,
 That vain it were her lids to close;
 So half-way from the bed she rose,
 And on her elbow did recline
 To look at the lady Geraldine.
 Beneath the lamp the lady bowed,

And slowly rolled her eyes around;
Then drawing in her breath aloud,
Like one that shuddered, she unbound
The cincture from beneath her breast:
Her silken robe, and inner vest,
Dropt to her feet, and full in view,
Behold! her bosom and half her side –
A sight to dream of, not to tell!
O shield her! shield sweet Christabel!

Yet Geraldine nor speaks nor stirs;
Ah! what a stricken look was hers!
Deep from within she seems half-way
To lift some weight with sick assay,
And eyes the maid and seeks delay;
Then suddenly, as one defied,
Collects herself in scorn and pride,
And lay down by the Maiden's side! –
And in her arms the maid she took, Ah wel-a-day!
And with low voice and doleful look
These words did say:

"In the touch of this bosom there worketh a spell,
Which is lord of thy utterance, Christabel!
Thou knowest to-night, and wilt know to-morrow,
This mark of my shame, this seal of my sorrow;
But vainly thou warrest,
For this is alone in
Thy power to declare,
That in the dim forest
Thou heard'st a low moaning,
And found'st a bright lady, surpassing fair;
And didst bring her home with thee in love and in charity,
To shield her and shelter her from the damp air."

LYRICAL ROMANTIC

Psyche

THE BUTTERFLY the ancient Grecians made
The soul's fair emblem, and its only name –
But of the soul, escaped the slavish trade
Of mortal life!—For in this earthly frame
Ours is the reptile's lot, much toil, much blame,
Manifold motions making little speed,
And to deform and kill the things whereon we feed.

COLERIDGE

The Pains of Sleep

ERE ON my bed my limbs I lay,
It hath not been my use to pray
With moving lips or bended knees;
But silently, by slow degrees,
My spirit I to Love compose,
In humble trust mine eye-lids close,
With reverential resignation,
No wish conceived, no thought exprest,
Only a sense of supplication;
A sense o'er all my soul imprest
That I am weak, yet not unblest,
Since in me, round me, every where
Eternal Strength and Wisdom are.

But yester-night I prayed aloud
In anguish and in agony,
Up-starting from the fiendish crowd
Of shapes and thoughts that tortured me:
A lurid light, a trampling throng,
Sense of intolerable wrong,
And whom I scorned, those only strong!
Thirst of revenge, the powerless will
Still baffled, and yet burning still!
Desire with loathing strangely mixed
On wild or hateful objects fixed.
Fantastic passions! maddening brawl!
And shame and terror over all!
Deeds to be hid which were not hid,
Which all confused I could not know
Whether I suffered, or I did:
For all seemed guilt, remorse or woe,

My own or others' still the same
Life-stifling fear, soul-stifling shame.

So two nights passed: the night's dismay
  Saddened and stunned the coming day.
  Sleep, the wide blessing, seemed to me
    Distemper's worst calamity.
The third night, when my own loud scream
  Had waked me from the fiendish dream,
O'ercome with sufferings strange and wild,
  I wept as I had been a child;
  And having thus by tears subdued
  My anguish to a milder mood,
  Such punishments, I said, were due
To natures deepliest stained with sin, –
  For aye entempesting anew
  The unfathomable hell within,
  The horror of their deeds to view,
To know and loathe, yet wish and do!
Such griefs with such men well agree,
But wherefore, wherefore fall on me?
  To be beloved is all I need,
  And whom I love, I love indeed.

Recollections of Love

I

HOW WARM this woodland wild Recess!
Love surely hath been breathing here;
And this sweet bed of heath, my dear!
Swells up, then sinks with faint caress,
    As if to have you yet more near.

II

Eight springs have flown, since last I lay
On sea-ward Quantock's healthy hills,
Where quiet sounds from hidden rills
Float here and there, like things astray,
And high o'er head the sky-lark shrills.

III

No voice as yet had made the air
Be music with your name; yet why
That asking look? that yearning sigh?
That sense of promise every where?
    Belovéd! flew your spirit by?

IV

As when a mother doth explore
The rose-mark on her long-lost child,
I met, I loved you, maiden mild!
As whom I long had loved before –
    So deeply had I been beguiled.

LYRICAL ROMANTIC

V

You stood before me like a thought,
A dream remembered in a dream.
But when those meek eyes first did seem
To tell me, Love within you wrought –
O Greta, dear domestic stream!

VI

Has not, since then, Love's prompture deep,
Has not Love's whisper evermore
Been ceaseless, as thy gentle roar?
Sole voice, when other voices sleep,
Dear under-song in clamour's hour.

Sonnet
TO THE RIVER OTTER

DEAR NATIVE Brook! wild Streamlet of the West!
  How many various-fated years have past,
What happy and what mournful hours, since last
  I skimm'd the smooth thin stone along thy breast,
Numbering its light leaps! yet so deep imprest
Sink the sweet scenes of childhood, that mine eyes
  I never shut amid the sunny ray,
But straight with all their tins thy waters rise,
Thy crossing plank, thy marge with willows grey,
And bedded sand that vein'd with various dyes
Gleam'd through thy bright transparence! On my way,
  Visions of Childhood! oft have ye beguil'd
Lone manhood's cares, yet waking fondest sighs:
  Ah! that once more I were a careless Child!

An Invocation

HEAR, SWEET Spirit, hear the spell.
Lest a blacker charm compel!
So shall the midnight breezes swell
With thy deep long-lingering knell.

And at evening evermore,
In a chapel on the shore,
Shall the chaunter, sad and saintly,
Yellow tapers burning faintly,
Doleful masses chaunt for thee,
Miserere Domine!

Hush! the cadence dies away
On the quiet moonlight sea;
The boatmen rest their oars and say,
Miserere Domine!

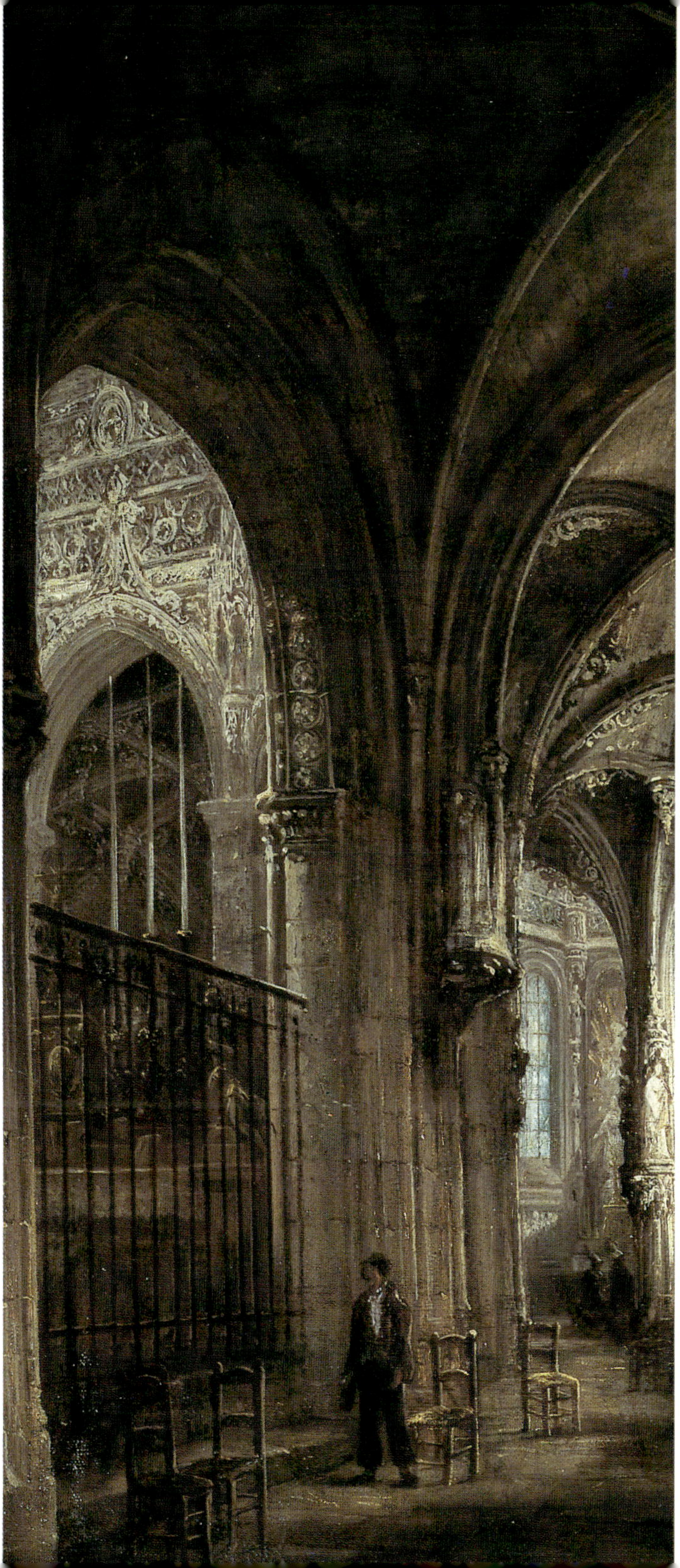

Genevieve

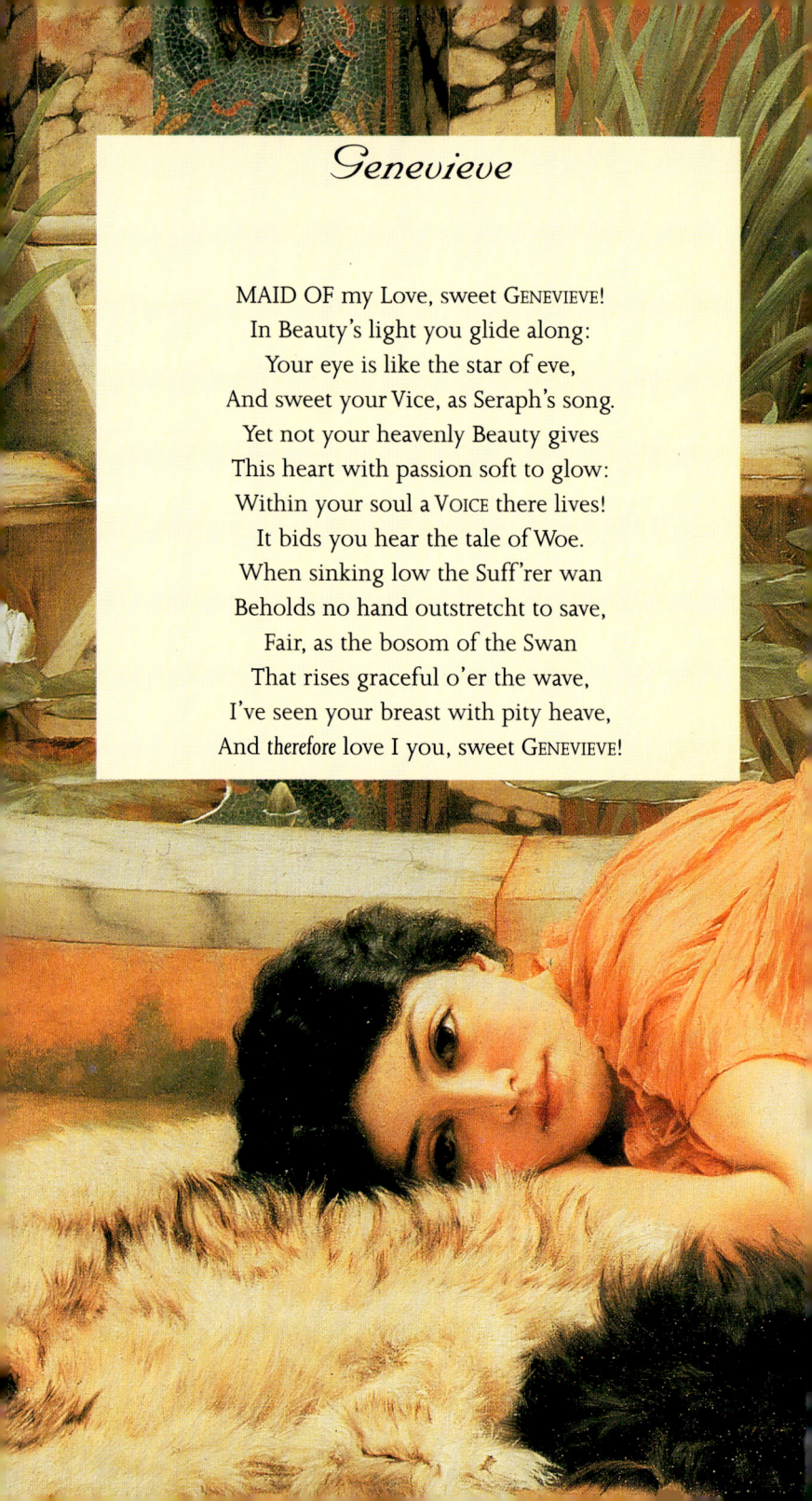

MAID OF my Love, sweet GENEVIEVE!
In Beauty's light you glide along:
Your eye is like the star of eve,
And sweet your Vice, as Seraph's song.
Yet not your heavenly Beauty gives
This heart with passion soft to glow:
Within your soul a VOICE there lives!
It bids you hear the tale of Woe.
When sinking low the Suff'rer wan
Beholds no hand outstretcht to save,
Fair, as the bosom of the Swan
That rises graceful o'er the wave,
I've seen your breast with pity heave,
And therefore love I you, sweet GENEVIEVE!

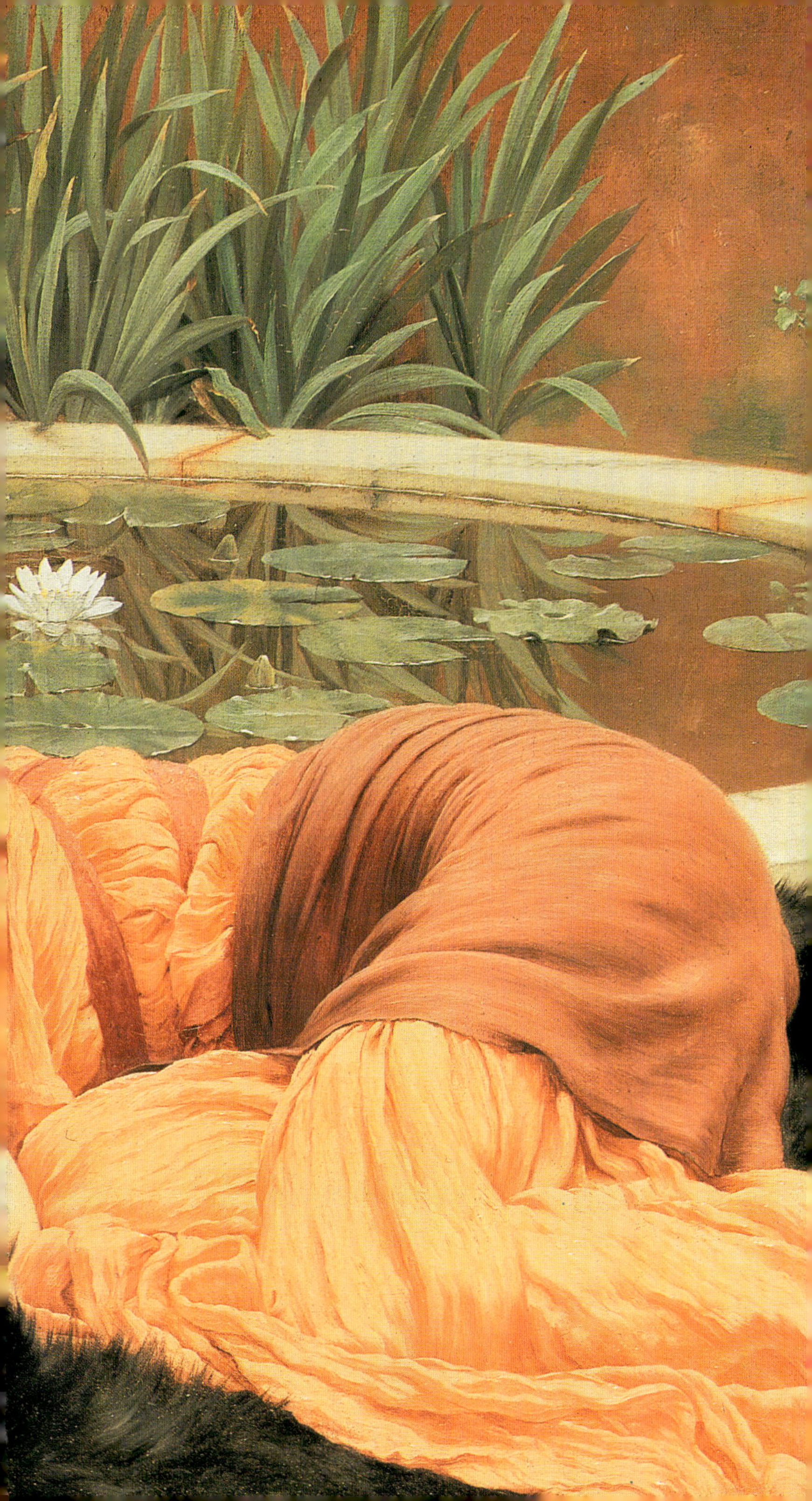

Epitaph

STOP, CHRISTIAN passer-by! – Stop, child of God,
And read with gentle breast. Beneath this sod
A poet lies, or that which once seem'd he.
O, lift one thought in prayer for S.T.C.;
That he who many a year with toil of breath
Found death in life, may here find life in death!
Mercy for praise – to be forgiven for fame
He ask'd, and hoped, through Christ. Do thou the same!

Desire

WHERE TRUE Love burns Desire is Love's pure flame;
It is the reflex of our earthly frame,
That takes its meaning from the nobler part,
And but translates the language of the heart.

Work Without Hope
LINES COMPOSED 21ST FEBRUARY 1825

ALL NATURE seems at work. Slugs leave their lair —
The bees are stirring — birds are on the wing —
And Winter slumbering in the open air,
Wears on his smiling face a dream of Spring!
And I the while, the sole unbusy thing,
Nor honey make, nor pair, nor build, nor wing.

Yet well I ken the banks where amaranths blow,
Have traced the fount whence streams of nectar flow.
Bloom, O ye amaranths! bloom for whom ye may,
For me ye bloom not! Glide, rich streams, away!
With lips unbrightened, wreathless brow, I stroll:
And would you learn the spells that drowse my soul?
Work without Hope draws nectar in a sieve,
And Hope without an object cannot live.

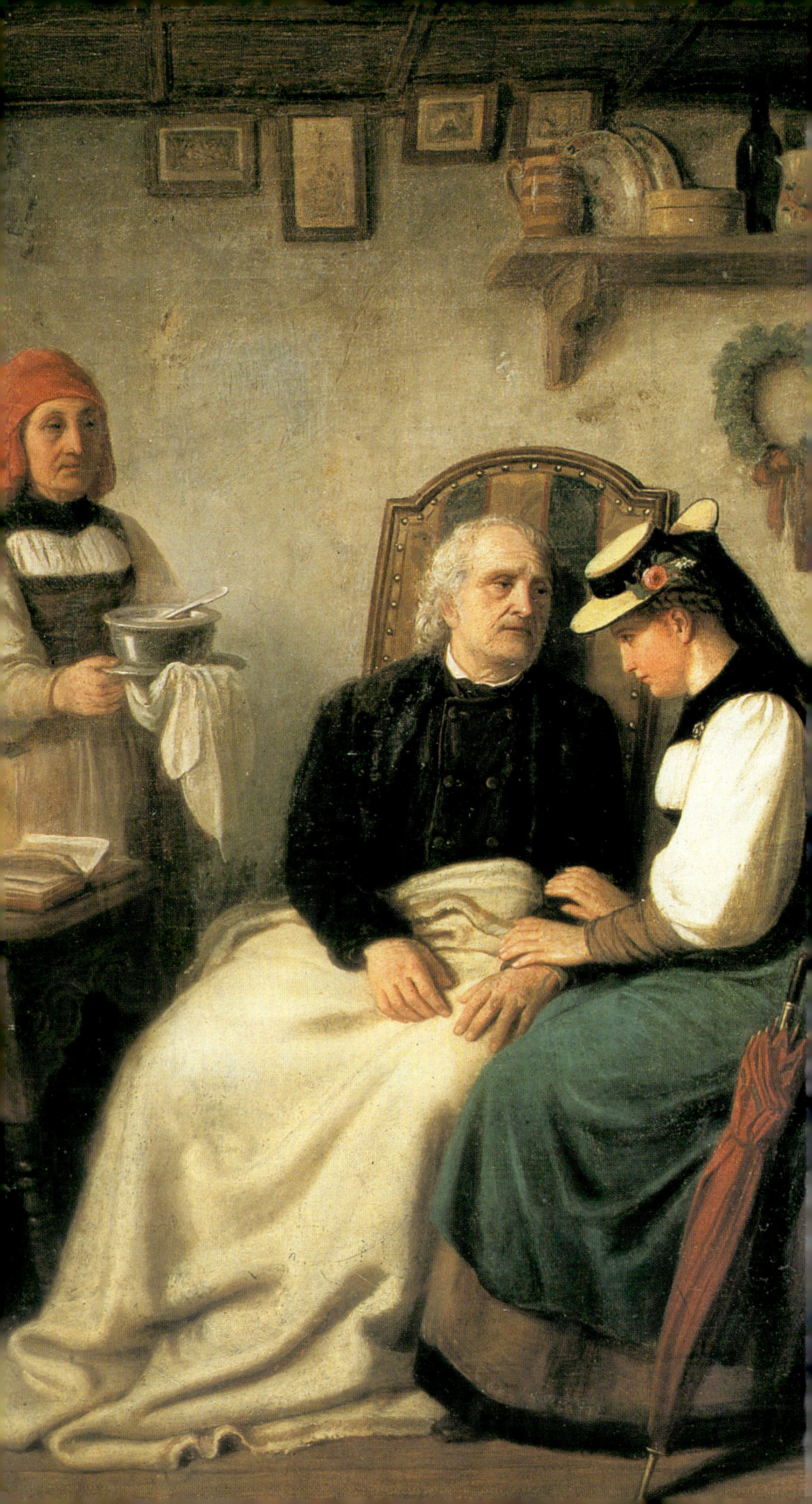

Lines on a Friend
WHO DIED OF A FRENZY FEVER INDUCED BY CALUMNIOUS REPORTS

EDMUND! THY grave with aking eye I scan,
And inly groan for Heaven's poor outcast, Man!
 'Tis tempest all or gloom: in early youth
 If gifted with the Ithuriel lance of Truth
 He force to start amid her feign'd caress
  Vice, siren-hag! in native ugliness,
 A Brother's fate will haply rouse the tear,
 And on he goes in heaviness and fear!
 But if his fond heart call to PLEASURE's bower
  Some pigmy FOLLY in a careless hour,
The faithless guest shall stamp th' inchanted ground
 And mingled forms of Mis'ry rise around:
 Heart-fretting FEAR, with pallid look aghast,
 That courts the future woe to hide the past:
 REMORSE, the poison'd arrow in his side
 And loud lewd MIRTH, to Anguish close allied:
 Till FRENZY, fierce-ey'd child of moping pain,
 Darts her hot lightning flash athwart the brain.

Rest, injur'd shade! Shall SLANDER squatting near
  Spit her cold venom in a DEAD MAN's ear?
  'Twas thine to feel the sympathetic glow
  In Merit's joy, and Poverty's meek woe;
  Thine all, that cheer the moment as it flies,
  The *zoneless* CARES, and Smiling COURTESIES.
 Nurs'd in thy heart the firmer Virtues grew,
 And in thy heart they wither'd! Such chill dew
 Wan INDOLENCE on each young blossom shed;
  And VANITY her filmy net-work spread,
  With eye that roll'd around in asking gaze,
 And tongue that traffick'd in the trade of praise.

Thy follies such! the hard world mark'd them well—
Were they more wise, the PROUD who never fell?
Rest, injur'd shade! the poor man's prayer of praise
On heaven-ward wing thy wounded soul shall raise.

As oft at twilight gloom thy grave I pass,
And sit me down upon its' recent grass,
With introverted eye I contemplate
Similitude of soul, perhaps of – Fate!
To me hath Heaven with bounteous hand assign'd
Energic Reason and a shaping mind,
The daring ken of Truth, the Patriot's part,
And Pity's sigh, that breathes the gentle heart –
Sloth-jaundic'd all! and from my graspless hand
Drop Friendship's precious pearls, like hour-glass and.
I weep, yet stoop not! the faint anguish flows,
A dreamy pang in Morning's fev'rish doze.

Is this pil'd Earth our Being's passless mound?
Till me, cold grave! is Death with poppies crown'd?
Tired Centinel! mid fitful starts I nod,
And fain would sleep, though pillow'd on a clod!

LYRICAL ROMANTIC

On Donne's Poetry

WITH DONNE, whose muse on dromedary trots,
Wreathe iron pokers into true-love knots;
Rhyme's sturdy cripple, fancy's maze and clue,
Wit's forge and fire-blast, meaning's press and screw.

Index to First Lines

All Nature seems at work. Slugs leave their lair 87

Dear native Brook! wild Streamlet of the West 81

Edmund! Thy grave with aking eye I scan 89
Ere on my bed my limbs I lay 76

Hear, sweet Spirit, hear the spell 82
How warm this woodland wild Recess 78

In Xanadu did Kubla Khan..56
It is an ancient Mariner 25

Maid of my Love, Sweet Genevieve 84
Mild Splendour of the various-vested Night 14

Once could the Morn's first beams, the healthful breeze 19

Sister of love-lorn Poets, Philomel 18
Stop, Christian passer-by! – Stop, child of God 86

'Tis the middle of night by the castle clock 64
The butterfly the ancient Grecians made 75
The Frost performs its secret ministry 60
Though veiled in spires of myrtle wreath 63

Verse, a breeze mid blossoms straying 16

We pledged our hearts, my love and I 59
Well, they are gone, and here must I remain 20
Where true Love burns Desire is Loves's pure flame 86
With Donne, whose muse on dromedary trots 91

LYRICAL ROMANTIC

Notes on Illustrations

3	Detail from *Samuel Taylor Coleridge*, by Peter Vandyke. Courtesy of The National Portrait Gallery, London.
5	*Furness Abbey, Lancashire*, by Thomas Hearne (Victoria & Albert, London). Courtesy of The Bridgeman Art Library.
7	*Samuel Taylor Coleridge*, by Peter Vandyke. Courtesy of The National Portrait Gallery, London.
12	*Lodore Derwentwater*, by Alfred de Breanski (Bonhams, London). Courtesy of The Bridgeman Art Library.
14-15	*A Moonlit Lake by a Castle*, by Joseph Wright of Derby (Christie's, London). Courtesy of The Bridgeman Art Library.
21	*The Orchard*, by Nelly Erichsen (Roy Miles Gallery, London). Courtesy of The Bridgeman Art Library.
24-5	*Shipping Scene*, by Thomas Sewell Robins (Oscar and Peter Johnson Ltd, London). Courtesy of The Bridgeman Art Library.
28	*On the Dogger Bank*, by William Clarkson Stanfield (Victoria & Albert Museum, London). Courtesy of The Bridgeman Art Library.
33	*Sailing Vessels in a Heavy Swell*, by François Etienne Musin (Christie's, London). Courtesy of The Bridgeman Art Library.
37	*The Shipwreck*, by Francis Danby (Wolverhampton Art Gallery, Staffordshire). Courtesy of The Bridgeman Art Library.
40-1	*The Shipwrecked Mariner*, by François Thomas-Louis Francia (Victoria & Albert Museum, London). Courtesy of The Bridgeman Art Library.
45	*Post Office Packet, 'Lady Hobart', Wrecked on an Iceberg*, by Nicholas Pocock (National Maritime Museum, London). Courtesy of The Bridgeman Art Library.
49	*Dead Calm – Sunset at the Bight of Exmouth*, by Francis Danby (Royal Albert Memorial Museum, Exeter). Courtesy of The Bridgeman Art Library.
54	*The Young Bride*, by Alcide Robaudi (Roy Miles Gallery, London). Courtesy of The Bridgeman Art Library.
57	*Outside the Mosque*, by Charles Robertson (Christie's, London), Courtesy of The Bridgeman Art Library.
61	*Repose*, by Alfred Provis (Beaton-Brown Fine Paintings, London). Courtesy of The Bridgeman Art Library.
65	*Britomart and Amoret*, by Mary F. Raphael (Christopher Wood Gallery, London). Courtesy of The Bridgeman Art Library.
70	*The Owl*, by Caspar-David Friedrich (Pushkin Museum, Moscow). Courtesy of The Bridgeman Art Library.
75	*Cupid and Psyche*, by Baron François Pascal Simon Gerard (Louvre, Paris). Courtesy of The Bridgeman Art Library.
79	*Windermere: From Orrest Head*, by James Baker Pyne (Dove Cottage Trust, Grasmere). Courtesy of The Bridgeman Art Library.
83	*Interior of the Church of St. Pierre, Caen*, by François d'Herbes (Musée Des Beaux Arts, Caen). Courtesy of The Bridgeman Art Library.
84-5	*Dolce Far Niente*, by John William Godward (Private Collection). Courtesy of The Bridgeman Art Library.
88	*The Elderly Invalid*, by Heinrich von Rustige (Josef Mensing Gallery, Hamm-Rhynern). Courtesy of The Bridgeman Art Library.
91	*Portrait of John Donne*, by Anonymous (Private Collection). Courtesy of The Bridgeman Art Library.
93	*A Girl with Flamingos*, by Arthur Drummond (Roy Miles Fine Paintings, London). Courtesy of The Bridgeman Art Library.
95	*View across Loch Awe, Argyllshire, to Kilchurn Castle and the Mountains Beyond*, by R.S. Barret (Victoria & Albert Museum, London). Courtesy of The Bridgeman Art Library.

LYRICAL ROMANTIC